TAKE A LEAF OUT OF GREGORY'S BOOK

by

Jack Bingham

Published by:
New Playwrights' Network
35 Sandringham Road
Macclesfield
Cheshire
SK10 1QB

ISBN 0 86319 214 9

CHARACTERS

MOTHER	REPORTER	MR BLACK
ELSIE	VICAR	MISS WHITE
CINDY	AGENT	MR GREEN
	MISS BROWN	

The characters in the third column are in the play throughout, under different guises, but played by the same four players. Each wears a costume of the appropriate colour all the time, and wears a coat and hat to differentiate each character. Thus, the Civil Servants wears bowlers and large hats, the Councillors, flat caps and small hats. The Police and Army, the appropriate caps and helmets.

The only permanent item on stage is a large tree, which goes up out of sight. The tree must be as realistic as possible and is centre stage. Down right is a table, consisting of two card tables pushed together, and four chairs. Leaning against the table is a large contour map, and across the top in large letters is written, 'ROAD PLANNING COMMITTEE'.

STAGE PLAN

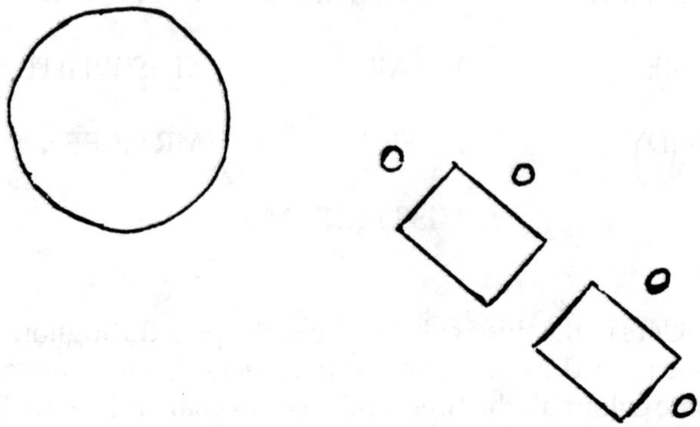

TAKE A LEAF OUT OF GREGORY'S BOOK

TAKE A LEAF OUT OF GREGORY'S BOOK

As the curtains open the phone is ringing. MISS WHITE runs on and picks up the phone.

WHITE: Hullo, this is the regional office of the Road Planning Committee, how can I help you?...*(Pauses, then puts down the phone and calls)* ...eh Mr Black, it's for you!

BLACK: *(Rushing on)* Who is it?

WHITE: *(Whispering)* The Ministry.

BLACK: *(Mouthing)* The Minister?...*(WHITE mouths 'yes')*...Good morning Minister...what?...oh...*(Mouths to WHITE 'it's not')*...indeed we are sir, in conference right at the moment...*(Signals to WHITE in a frantic manner)*...hard at it, sir, I do assure you...*(White rushes out and back again with a notebook and pencil. She sits)*...what's that sir?...I'll check right away sir...*(GREEN and BROWN rush on, clutching files, and sit)*...no sir, right now...*(Puts his hand over the phone and hisses at WHITE)*...how long have we been meeting?

WHITE: *(Confused)* About six months, Fridays at my flat don't you remember?

BLACK: Roughly six months sir...*(Hand over phone again)*...no, no, no, no...this committee?

WHITE: Oh, about five and a half years, I think?...*(Looks at GREEN and BROWN who both shrug)*

BLACK: Five and a half years sir...what's that sir?...yes sir, I understand...right away sir...*(Puts down the phone and sits)*

GREEN: Well?

BLACK: He wants the plans for the new ring road to be on his desk by tomorrow.

BROWN: Tomorrow?

GREEN: Rushing things a bit aren't they?

BLACK: You heard me tell him, five and a half years.

BROWN: Surely he knows that the normal length of time allowed for such committees is seven years?

GREEN: I mean, how are we to be expected to reach such a decision in so short a time?

BLACK: I suppose we'll have to do something.

GREEN: Damned bad form, what?

BROWN: Oh, I agree.

BLACK: Well, let's get on with it, shall we?

WHITE: Now?

BLACK: 'Fraid so...*(Stands and picks up the map and stands it on the table. They all look at it earnestly)*...any ideas?...anyone?

BROWN: Is this the right way up, do you think?

BLACK: *(Peering closely at the map)* Do you know, I think you're right...*(Turns the map round)*...there, that's better.

BROWN: So, what do we do now?

BLACK: Well, I should have thought that was obvious...*(They all look at him and the map, blankly)*...we plan the road.

GREEN: Oh...how about a straight line, right up the middle?

BLACK: *(Draws his finger down the map)* Like that, you mean?

GREEN: That's the ticket, I was always fond of a good straight line.

BLACK: Something to do with your public school upbringing, no doubt?

GREEN: That, and Nanny...*(Stands)*...well, if that's it?...

BROWN: Perhaps?...*(GREEN sits)*...perhaps not quite so straight?...angled somewhat?

BLACK: *(Drawing his finger diagonally)* Like that, do you mean?

BROWN: That's much better, I think.

WHITE: Doesn't seem quite so clinical.

BLACK: Very well...all those in favour?...*(They all raise their hands. BLACK takes a red felt tip pen and draws a diagonal line down the map)*

BROWN: Has character, that line.

WHITE: Beautifully drawn, of course.

BLACK: Thank you...*(They all stand and start to move off)*

GREEN: *(Peering closely at the map)* I say, hang on a bit.

BLACK: Something wrong?

GREEN: That line.

BLACK: Yes?

GREEN: You know, it goes slap bang through some property that my aunt owns.

BLACK: Oh dear, can't have that sort of thing, can we?... let's see...if we draw the line on the other angle?...*(Peers closely)* Anyone know anyone at...where is it...Chapelstow?

BROWN: No.

GREEN: Not me.

WHITE: Nor me.

BLACK: Good, that's settled then...*(Draws the line)* Not bad that, for five and a half years planning, is it?

GREEN: It most certainly isn't, and now perhaps we can carry on with what we were doing.

BLACK: By all means.

WHITE: Where were we?

GREEN: You had bid two spades.

BROWN: And I had doubled.

BLACK: Who's dummy?

GREEN: Me.

BLACK: Well, perhaps you might nip round to the Minister's office and tell him the good news?

GREEN: Righto...*(He picks up the map and exits)*

WHITE: I have another idea, why don't we take the phone off the hook?

BLACK: Why?

WHITE: All this ringing interferes with the game.

BROWN: Good thinking.

BLACK: I've a better idea...*(He pulls the cord of the phone away and they all exit)*

(ELSIE enters and takes one of the tables to the other side of the stage)

ELSIE: Shall I lay breakfast Mum?

MOTHER: *(Off)* No, not yet...Gregory!...*(Enters with table-cloth and cutlery)* That brother of yours, he'll be late for his own funeral, I swear.

ELSIE: Mum!

MOTHER: What?

ELSIE: You forgot again.

MOTHER: What?

ELSIE: He's married now...perhaps they?...

MOTHER: What?
ELSIE: You know?
MOTHER: Oh yes, of course, I forgot again, didn't I...?

(They both start to lay the table)

ELSIE: He's been married two years Mum.
MOTHER: My memory...*(Calls automatically)* Gregory!
ELSIE: Mum!
MOTHER: Oh dear...*(Whispers loudly)* Gregory, your breakfast is nearly ready.
ELSIE: Don't forget to call Cindy.
MOTHER: Who?
ELSIE: Cindy, the girl he married.
MOTHER: *(Calls loudly)* Cindy, your...
CINDY: *(Muttering)* What?
MOTHER: Breakfast is nearly ready, dear.
CINDY: *(Sitting)* Where's Greg?
MOTHER: Don't you know?
CINDY: Haven't seen him.
MOTHER: He went to bed last night?
CINDY: Oh yes.
MOTHER: And he's not there now?
CINDY: No.
ELSIE: I wonder where he can be?
MOTHER: If you've lost him.
CINDY: Oh, I hope I haven't done that.
ELSIE: I bet you do.
MOTHER: Elsie, that is quite enough of that, thank you!
CINDY: I remember he got up in the middle of the night.
MOTHER: And?
CINDY: Nothing.
MOTHER: Nothing at all?
CINDY: No.
MOTHER: He must have got up for something...he always did as a child.
ELSIE: Not the same thing I bet.
MOTHER: Elsie!
ELSIE: Well...
CINDY: I pretended to go to sleep again, and watched. He got dressed and went out.
MOTHER: Strange.
CINDY: I got up and looked out of the window and saw him go down to the shed.
MOTHER: The shed?
CINDY: And after a while he came out with a rope, a saw and an old orange

box.

MOTHER: How funny.

CINDY: I thought perhaps he was going to make something.

MOTHER: In the middle of the night?

CINDY: You never know.

ELSIE: I wonder where he can be?

BLACKOUT. The three women clear the table and exit. Lights up on the other table with BLACK, WHITE, BROWN and GREEN sitting round.

BLACK: *(Knocking on the table)* Special meeting of the town council now in session.

WHITE: Why are we meeting?

BLACK: If you will be patient.

GREEN: To discuss the Government plan to put the new road right through the middle of the town.

BLACK: As I was going to say...

GREEN: I hope that explains.

WHITE: Yes thank you, Mr Green.

BLACK: *(Quietly mimicking)* Oh yes, thank you, Mr Green.

BROWN: Well, what are we going to do about it?

BLACK: I think...

GREEN: A petition, at least.

WHITE: What a good idea.

BLACK: I was going to say that.

REPORTER: *(Rushing in)* Can I have a statement!

GREEN:)
BLACK:) Certainly!

BLACK: Just a moment, who's the bloody chairman?

WHITE: You are Arthur.

BLACK: So who's in bloody charge?

WHITE: You are Arthur?

BLACK: So I'll give the bloody statement...*(Pause)* What statement?

REPORTER: Concerning the efforts of Mr Gregory Kerslake, assistant plasterer of 14, Chestnut Avenue.

WHITE: *(Writing)* Why, is he some sort of flasher?

REPORTER: No, nothing like that, at all.

WHITE: *(Scratching out the writing)* Pity.

GREEN: What's he done?

REPORTER: *(Reading)*"At six o'clock last night, the Ministry announced that a new ring road has been planned to go right through the centre of a small town, called, Chapelstow".

BLACK: Well, we know all that, that's the precise reason why we're here.

REPORTER: "The town has an ancient monument, situated in the High Street, a seven hundred year old tree, a rare oak breed. The road, as planned, will destroy this monument to a past age. The Ministry have stated that there is no viable or economic way, that the road can be built any where else..."

BROWN: Look, we know all this...

REPORTER: "...at four o'clock this morning, 23 year old Gregory Kerslake, a local man, climbed the tree..."

BROWN: We didn't know that.

REPORTER: "...He sawed away all the lower branches, and has made his home in the upper part of the tree. The only way up is by a rope, which he lowers when required. He intends to stay there, as a protest, until the road is moved elsewhere!.

BLACK: *(Pause)* Bloody hell!

REPORTER: *(Writing)* Mr Black, honest and forthright town councillor, was quoted as saying that the efforts of Mr Kerslake would be supported, to the hilt, by all of the townspeople.

BROWN: Well, I think that the whole thing is preposterous, and that the man must be mad if he thinks he can halt progress by such crude methods,

REPORTER: *(Writing)* Miss Brown, outspoken champion of lost causes said, 'Bloody hell'.

BROWN: I did not.

REPORTER: Believe me, much better for your image.

BROWN: Is it?

REPORTER: Much better.

BROWN: Thank you.

REPORTER: My pleasure, all part of the local service. We are thinking of doing a series on the subject, with eye catching titles on the tree theme. Such as 'Gregory branches out' or 'Do you twig what Gregory is doing'.

WHITE: What a good idea.

GREEN: How about, 'He goes up a trunk, to stop a trunk'.

REPORTER: Smacks rather of Tarzan, that.

BLACK: 'Gregory's bark is worse than his bite'.

REPORTER: Has possibilities.

BROWN: 'Gregory gets to the root of the matter'.

REPORTER: You're getting the idea, we have also thought of a campaign slogan.

WHITE: Campaign?...what Campaign?

REPORTER: The campaign, sponsored by the local paper of course, to oppose the road, are you in favour?

BLACK: Most certainly.

REPORTER: The slogan is 'Take a leaf out of Gregory's book and oppose the road'.

BLACK: Oh, I like that, I do. Why don't we have a badge of some sort, which people can buy, and money goes to the funds for the campaign.

WHITE: Splendid!

BLACK: We could have the badge printed in the shape of an oak leaf, with the words, 'Oppose the road', right across.

GREEN: Your brother has a printing works, hasn't he?

BLACK: What?...why, so he has!

GREEN: I thought so.

BLACK: So what?

GREEN: I should have thought a far more permanent badge could be made, in metal, with a leaf motif. Something to be kept, as a momento of this historic campaign.

WHITE: Your father has a factory that makes small metal toys, hasn't he?

GREEN: I don't see what that has to do with it?

WHITE: Oh no?

BROWN: And would your father be willing to make these badges at a reduced cost?

GREEN: Would his brother?

REPORTER: Ladies, gentlemen...should such thoughts be in our minds at this moment?

BROWN: You're right.

REPORTER: Besides, we haven't got that much time to decide.

WHITE: Oh?

REPORTER: Well, the nationals are bound to pick up the story, and bang go my exclusive rights. *(He exits)*

BLACK: We shall split into two groups and one will deal with the campaign, and the other with the publicity...*(They all stand)*...there's no time to be wasted. We meet again tomorrow.

(They all rush off in different directions. MOTHER, ELSIE and CINDY walk on to the centre of the stage, stand in front of the tree and gaze up)

MOTHER: I can't see him.

ELSIE: It's ever so high, isn't it?

MOTHER: I do hope he's all right up there.

ELSIE: They say it's over seven hundred years old.

MOTHER: Fancy that.

(Pause)

CINDY: I wonder when its birthday is?

MOTHER: You can tell by the rings, can't you?

CINDY: Oh, that's nice.

ELSIE: What is?

CINDY: Giving a tree a ring for its birthday...I wonder where they are?

ELSIE: *(Pointing up and shouting)* There!...

CINDY: The rings?...where?

ELSIE: No, Gregory, he's up there.

MOTHER: Well, we all know that.

ELSIE: I saw a shoe.

(CINDY begins to snivel all through the scene)

MOTHER: A shoe?...what colour?

ELSIE: Couldn't tell.

MOTHER: If he's got his best shoes on I'll...Gregory!...Gregory!...can you hear me?...*(There is a muffled reply and no word can be distinguished. This is repeated throughout the rest of the play and signified by 'VOICE')*...what?...*(VOICE)*...no, I don't think so, dear.

ELSIE: What did he say?

MOTHER: Something about the reporters being here...*(VOICE)* you're very feint dear...no dear, she's crying...*(Louder sobs from CINDY)*...I don't know, I think it's something to do with the trees birthday.

ELSIE: Oh Mum.

MOTHER: What now?

ELSIE: Well, you know...it was when I mentioned the shoes, that's what did it.

MOTHER: Was it?...*(She pats CINDY on the shoulder)* There, there, my love, don't you fret, he probably hasn't got his best shoes on after all. *(Louder sobs)*

ELSIE: Mum, she's missing Greg.

MOTHER: Yes, I suppose she must be...but could you sob a little less loudly, I'm trying to hear what Gregory wants...*(VOICE)*...you what?...*(VOICE)*...he's lowering the rope...*(A rope comes down with a note attached)*

ELSIE: There's the note.

MOTHER: *(Reading)* He wants all these things on the list to be sent up to him. He says if we come back when it's dark, he'll lower the orange box and we can put them in that. That way, no one will ever know he's being supplied with food, and will think he's fasting. This will help his protest, he says.

ELSIE: *(Looking over her shoulder)* What on earth does he want these things for?

MOTHER: That's a point...*(Calls)* Gregory, what are you doing up there?

ELSIE: He's probably got a good reason.

MOTHER: He'd better have.

REPORTER: *(Rushing in)* Where is he?

MOTHER: Who?

REPORTER: Him!...thingy!

MOTHER: Up there.

(The rope is dissappearing and the REPORTER makes a despairing jump at it)

REPORTER: Damn!...*(Calls)* Can I have a word with you! *(VOICE)*...he's very rude, isn't he?

ELSIE: Nervous, I expect.

MOTHER: *(Calls)* This man is a reporter, dear...*(VOICE)*...yes, that's right...*(VOICE)*...the local paper.

REPORTER: *(Calls)* But I can get it into the nationals, no problem, and we're organising a big campaign to help.

ELSIE: He's gone quiet.

REPORTER: By the way, who are you people?

ELSIE: His sister.

MOTHER: I'm his mother.

REPORTER: What about her?

ELSIE: That's his wife.

REPORTER: Ah...I wonder if I might have a word with you, Mrs Kerslake?

MOTHER: Certainly.

REPORTER: No, I meant that Mrs Kerslake, human angle, personal and all that.

MOTHER: But I'm his mother!

REPORTER: Another time, maybe...*(He leads CINDY off)*

MOTHER: Well, really!

ELSIE: Never mind, Mum, it's Gregory we should be thinking of now.

MOTHER: All the same.

ELSIE: *(Calls)* See you later Greg!

MOTHER: Yes, and take care of yourself dear...*(They start to go off)* I wonder what he really wants those things for?

(Lights down. COUNCILLOR BROWN and GREEN (Civil Servants) sit down at the table right)

BROWN: So that's the story, this fool of a man is up the tree and will not come down.

GREEN: Is there no way of shifting him?

BROWN: Not without a great deal of fuss, and publicity. The whole town is behind him, They don't want the road, either.

GREEN: That's all very well, but I have a lot of connections who are relying on this road being completed. If it is, then they make a good deal of profit, and if they do, so do we...I trust you understand?

BROWN: Oh yes, very much so.

GREEN: We cannot afford publicity, so you'll have to think of something. What about the police?

BROWN: He's committing no crime.

GREEN: All the same, you'd better try.

BROWN: Very well...good bye.

GREEN: Good bye.

(GREEN exits and BROWN dials a number on the phone. The phone on the table on the other side of the stage rings. P.C. BLACK enters and answers)

BLACK: Hullo, hullo, hullo.

BROWN: Is that the police?

BLACK: Madam, did I not say, 'hullo, hullo, hullo'?

BROWN: You did.

BLACK: Then you know surely that all policemen say 'hullo, hullo, hullo'? Then this must be the police station, I'm afraid you'll have to be somewhat quicker than that, madam.

BROWN: I'll try.

BLACK: You see, we are trying to cultivate a happier image, back to the jolly policeman type, you know?

BROWN: I'm so glad.

BLACK: A little joke to get you into that happy frame of mind...do you know why policeman have bigger balls than firemen?

BROWN: I haven't the faintest idea.

BLACK: Because they sell more tickets.

BROWN: If you could possibly spare a minute?

BLACK: Certainly madam, anything to assist the public.

BROWN: I wish to report an obstruction.

BLACK: Have you tried a laxative?

BROWN: Look, I accept the fact that the police are a jolly lot, and I am very pleased, but can we please get on with the serious business?

BLACK: I'm sorry madam, I have my pencil poised at the ready, the notebook is spotless, and I have my serious face on.

BROWN: Very well...there is a man up a tree, and I wish him to be removed.

BLACK: *(Pause)* You did say this was serious?

BROWN: I did.

BLACK: Then I suggest that you contact the fire brigade, as they rescue cats from trees and I'm certain they can manage a man.

BROWN: I don't think that you quite understand.

BLACK: I'm damned sure I don't.

BROWN: This man is living up in the tree.

BLACK: You said that he was causing an obstruction.

BROWN: He is.

BLACK: Yes.

BLACK: Madam, I feel that I should point out that only the odd sparrow or blackbird could seriously object to him living in a tree.

BROWN: But he is a nuisance.

BLACK: Ah, now that is different.

BROWN: How?

BLACK: If he is creating a nuisance, then that could be construed as a criminal act, and that way, madam, we can have him, and rest assured, we will. Can I please have your name, madam?

BROWN: This is an anonymous call.

BLACK: An anonymous call?...oh goody, my first ever, can I have your name and address?

BROWN: I am Miss Brown of the Chapelstow council.
BLACK: Thank you, we'll look into this.
BROWN: Thank you.

(They both put down their phones and BROWN exits)

BLACK: *(Calls)* Sergeant!
WHITE: *(Entering)* What is it now?
BLACK: Another crank call.
WHITE: Anonymous I suppose?
BLACK: That's right.
WHITE: Who was it this time?
BLACK: Councillor Brown.
WHITE: Again?...that's her fourth anonymous call this month, isn't it?
BLACK: Right again, sergeant.
WHITE: And what was it this time?
BLACK: A man living in a tree.
WHITE: Well, that's new at least.
BLACK: Do we investigate?
WHITE: What's the weather like?
BLACK: Sunny.
WHITE: Then let's go for a walk.
BLACK: To Chapelstow?
WHITE: Why not, it's a lovely day.

(They put their arms round each other and skip off. The lights dim. ELSIE, MOTHER and CINDY enter, carrying a loaded orange box between them. They get to the tree, put down the box and ELSIE gives a piercing whistle. The rope comes down, and they attach the box to it. They tug on the rope and it is hauled back up. They all wave goodbye and tiptoe off. After a pause the REPORTER appears from the side, backing slowly to the tree, which he circles warily. From the other side another man appears doing the same thing. They come face to face in the dim light)

REPORTER: Who's there!
AGENT: What?
REPORTER: Don't move, I'm a karate expert.
AGENT: And I've got cats eyes.
REPORTER: Oh no you haven't.
AGENT: I tell you I have.
REPORTER: All right then, how many fingers am I holding up?
AGENT: Two.
REPORTER: Here, how do you know that?
AGENT: 'Cos that's all people ever hold up to me.
REPORTER: Right, so you haven't got cats eyes?
AGENT: I have, I have, I've got a lorry load down the road, in the bushes. Mate

of mine is in the road contracting business and lets me have them wholesale...you want to buy some?

REPORTER: No thank you, wouldn't know what to do with them...who are you anyway?

AGENT: I'm an agent.

REPORTER: For what?

AGENT: Anything.

REPORTER: Anything?

AGENT: There are always people around, who want things done, and don't have the faintest idea on how to go about it.

REPORTER: Such as?

AGENT: You, for instance.

REPORTER: Me?

AGENT: Yes, you...maybe I can help you. Why are you creeping round a tree, in the dead of night?

REPORTER: I'm after a story.

AGENT: Ah, reporter, are you?

REPORTER: Yes.

AGENT: And you want to talk to the geezer, up the tree?

REPORTER: Are you his agent?

AGENT: I am now.

REPORTER: Right, I want an interview.

AGENT: And you've come to the right person...you see what I mean?

REPORTER: Can you fix it?

AGENT: Can I?...leave it to me, my son, no trouble at all.

REPORTER: Tomorrow?

AGENT: Tomorrow it is.

REPORTER: Thanks a lot...*(He exits)*

AGENT: Nothing to it...trouble is, what about him up there...*(Calls)* Oi!, you up there!...*(Silence)*...Now listen to me, my son, I could do you a power of good, get this protest off the ground...well, it's off the ground at the moment, I know, but I have contacts, capice?...*(VOICE)*...what's that?...right, you're on. I'll see you tomorrow...*(He exits)*

(Blackout. Lights up next morning. P.C. BLACK enters putting on his helmet and straightening his tie. INSPECTOR GREEN enters from the other side)

GREEN: Constable!

BLACK: Oh...good morning, sir.

GREEN: What are you doing here?

BLACK: Er...on surveillance, sir.

GREEN: In the bushes?

BLACK: Well...where better to surveill?...that is sir...we have reason to believe...

GREEN: Yes?

BLACK: We have been given to understand...
GREEN: What?
BLACK: What are you doing here, anyway?
GREEN: You're not supposed to ask me questions like that.
BLACK: Why not?

(Sergeant WHITE enters from the same side as BLACK. She is patting her hair in place and straightening her skirt)

GREEN: Sergeant!
WHITE: Oh!

(Sergeant BROWN enters from the other side also patting her hair and straightening her skirt)

BROWN: Yes, dear?
WHITE: Oh.
BROWN: Oh.
GREEN: Oh.
BLACK: I wonder if I might have a quiet word with you, sir?
GREEN: A reasonable request, constable...*(They retreat to one side of the stage as the two sergeants go to the other, eyeing each other, warily)*
WHITE: Inspector now, is it?
BROWN: You noticed?
WHITE: Rather ostentatious...I do hope that his pips didn't get in the way?
BROWN: Still with the other ranks, I see?
WHITE: It has it's compensations.
BROWN: Really?
WHITE: I can always give the orders.
BROWN: I hadn't thought about that.
GREEN: *(Coming back to the women, with BLACK)* Right, that's settled then.
BROWN: What is?
GREEN: Never you mind. Now, let us get on with the investigation.
BROWN: What investigation?
GREEN: The reason that we are all here, sergeant, the investigation into the intruder in the tree.

(They all gaze up and slowly circle the tree)

BLACK: Anyone see him?
WHITE: No.
GREEN: Give him a hail, constable.
BLACK: *(Calls)* You up there, can you hear me!... *(VOICE)* we seem to have made contact, sir.
GREEN: Very good...carry on.

BLACK: *(Calls)* We would like to have words with you sir!...*(VOICE)* We?...we're the police...*(A cabbage is dropped)* do you mind, there's no need to take that attitude.

BROWN: I would say that that action, constitutes an assault with a deadly weapon.

GREEN: A deadly weapon?

WHITE: She would know all about them, sir.

BROWN: In those circumstances, sir, we are quite within our rights to remove him.

GREEN: Extremely good thinking, sergeant.

BLACK: Just a moment sir, he's saying something...*(VOICE)*...that's all very well you being sorry, but it's a bit late now, isn't it?

GREEN: Arrest him constable.

BLACK: We're coming up after you, sonny...*(VOICE)*...what's that?....*(VOICE goes on for a long time. Pause. BLACK slowly comes over to the others)*

GREEN: Well?

BLACK: He has brought up, sir, a rather pertinent and tricky argument, sir.

GREEN: The man is causing an obstruction.

WHITE: And what's more, we've had an official complaint.

BROWN: Have you?

GREEN: Who from?

WHITE: An anonymous caller.

GREEN: Really?...who was it?

WHITE: A Miss Brown from Chapelstow.

GREEN: I never get any anonymous calls, it's not fair.

BLACK: If I may interrupt, sir?

GREEN: Oh very well, if you must, but I'm beginning to find all this just a tiny bit boring.

BLACK: The man in the tree has broached an academic argument, which, if analysed, could conceivably alter the whole concept of our investigation.

GREEN: Pardon?

BLACK: We, sir, are in schtuck.

GREEN: How?

BLACK: The man has pointed out that from his perch up there, he has an uninterrupted view of the surrounded countryside.

GREEN: I dare say he has.

BLACK: Also, he can see whatever goes on, directly underneath the tree.

GREEN: I don't dispute that.

BLACK: Also, whatever goes on, in the bushes, either side of the tree.

GREEN: Oh.

WHITE: Oh.

BROWN: Oh.

BLACK: Oh, indeed.

(There is a long silence)

WHITE: I can't see that he's doing any real harm up there, sir.
BROWN: I agree, and what is more, he is doing it for a very worthwhile cause.
BLACK: Myself, I don't believe he is contravening a single law.
GREEN: Thank you for your opinions, which I have carefully considered, and after careful consideration, I am inclined to agree with your remarks.
WHITE: May I point out, sir, that this complaint was made by an anonymous caller.
GREEN: Now, that is something that ought to be investigated.
BROWN: I absolutely agree, sir.
WHITE: We'll get on to that right away, sir.
GREEN: Good thinking sergeant.
WHITE: Coming, constable?
BLACK: Right away.

(They all wave to each other and exit. The AGENT appears from behind the tree)

AGENT: Very good, my son, you're learning. Now, how about me coming up there...to see you...*(SILENCE)*... Look, we could be good for each other. I've got some ideas that'll knock you cold...how about it?... *(Pause, then the rope is slowly lowered. The AGENT winds it round himself and is about to climb up as the lights go out. Lights up as quickly as possible as the AGENT produces a 'Branch' from behind the tree and sits to one side. The Vicar is behind the tree the other side, on a higher perch. When he appears, it is his head only that is seen. AGENT sitting)* God, there must be an easier way up than that, I'm knackered...*(Looks around)* Well, show yourself then!
VICAR: *(Appearing round the trunk)* Can I be of some assistance?
AGENT: *(Jumping up)* Jesus Christ, where did you come from?
VICAR: I feel that should be the other way round.
AGENT: What?
VICAR: If you had said, 'Have you come from Jesus Christ', then the answer would have to be 'yes'.
AGENT: Now look, Gregory, you startled me, I didn't know you were a sky pilot. That puts an entirely different light on the subject, know what I mean?
VICAR: But I'm not Gregory.
AGENT: You're not?
VICAR: I'm the vicar.
AGENT: Well, that's a surprise.
VICAR: *(Pointing up)* Gregory's up there.
AGENT: Dead?
VICAR: One branch higher.
AGENT: Why?
VICAR: Basically, he's a very insecure person.

AGENT: I'm not surprised, I'm none too happy myself, up here.

VICAR: He's very shy.

AGENT: Well, I've got business with him.

VICAR: Really?

AGENT: What are you doing up here anyway?

VICAR: It's quite simple you see, the other night, before Gregory made his historic climb, I was bird watching.

AGENT: Oh yeah?

VICAR: There had been strong reports of nightjars in the vicinity.

AGENT: Get away?

VICAR: The night vigil was long and I fell asleep, in the crock of the tree. When I awoke, Gregory had completed his coup, and I was stranded.

AGENT: You can get down now.

VICAR: I don't want to now, he's doing such a grand job.

AGENT: I'm his agent.

VICAR: He's very frightened of strangers.

AGENT: I'm not a stranger, I'm his friend...can I talk to him?

VICAR: Perhaps I can be of assistance there, as I have managed to get through to him, on occasions...*(Calls quietly)* Gregory, oh Gregory, there's someone here to see you...*(VOICE)*...you cannot hide for ever, Gregory, for as our Good Lord said...*(VOICE)*...and kindly do not interrupt...*(VOICE)* He's a trifle fragile this morning.

AGENT: Let me have a go... *(calls)* Look, my son, don't be scared, I'm on your side. I can organise things, make things happen, make it big, that's what you want, isn't it? All I ask, is a little something to tide me over, just expenses...say...50%...*(silence)*

VICAR: I'm afraid that you have touched upon his deep sense of anti-materialism.

AGENT: That's not all I'll touch if I get my hands on him.

VICAR: Perhaps?...

AGENT: Yes?

VICAR: I could act as his spokesman, a go-between?

AGENT: Eh?

VICAR: In these troubled first few hours, I have calmed his restless soul. I have offered comfort in words, and he has come to look upon me as his mentor in things spiritual, and material. He firmly believes in the Divinity.

AGENT: How much?

VICAR: 25%.

AGENT: You're on.

VICAR: Right.

AGENT: The first thing we have to do is to get some rallies going, get the people here.

VICAR: Why?

AGENT: The more people there are, the more business I can do. I've got contacts with the ice-cream boys, hot-dogs, and drinks concessions, we'll make a bomb.

VICAR: It sounds most enterprising.

AGENT: I've got it!

VICAR: *(Making a 'cross')* What?

AGENT: You.

VICAR: Me?

AGENT: Every Sunday we'll have a service, a church service.

VICAR: You mean here?...in the tree?

AGENT: This will be...what do you call it?

VICAR: Pulpit?

AGENT: That's it, pulpit...we'll call it 'The pulpit in the tree'. We'll have floodlights and loudspeakers.

VICAR: Sounds most enterprising...I could have a closer relationship with God up here.

AGENT: More than likely, old son, but what's more important, think of the collection, down there.

VICAR: We'll milk'em rotten..*(voice)* yes, Gregory?..*(voice)*..he wants to know about the protest.

AGENT: Big, very big Greg...tell him it'll be very big.

VICAR: *(Calls)* Very big, Gregory!

AGENT: Perhaps I'd better leave?

VICAR: Leave things to me.

AGENT: I'll be seeing you.

(Blackout. Lights up on the stage. In the centre the tables are set together, with two chairs either side. The branch is struck. INSPECTOR GREEN is seated. COUNCILLOR BROWN and Civil Servants, BLACK and WHITE enter)

BLACK: Inspector Green?

GREEN: At your service.

BLACK: Black, from the Ministry.

GREEN: How do you do?

BLACK: My secretary, Miss White, and this is Miss Brown from the local council.

GREEN: Not the anonymous caller?

BROWN: That's me.

GREEN: I've been dying to meet you, Miss Brown, please come and sit by me.

BROWN: *(Sitting)* Thank you.

GREEN: And if you two will sit on the other side?

BLACK: *(Sitting)* May we begin?

GREEN: Ready when you are, squire.

BLACK: The problem is simple...the Ministry wish this road to go through the town, and Miss Brown here, represents the faction that supports that idea.

GREEN: But I thought the council were against it?

BROWN: Not all of us feel that way, there are those that feel that the road could mean prosperity.

BLACK: And there are other factors.

GREEN: *(Whipping on a bowler hat)* I'll say there are...*(changing to police cap)* I see. I trust that you are not attempting to influence me?...*(bowler)*...Not at all...*(cap)*...bribe?...*(bowler)*...oh no!...*(cap)*...that's all right then.

BLACK: Sorted out?

GREEN: Yes, thank you.

BLACK: The point is this, that road was planned after a great deal of research, and years of labour...

WHITE: Hear hear!

BLACK: ...and must go through. The man in the tree is obstructing the course of progress.

BROWN: He must be removed.

GREEN: That may cause a problem or two.

BLACK: I don't see why.

GREEN: He has certain rights, you know.

WHITE: Rights?

GREEN: The rights of an ordinary citizen to protest, providing that they commit no crime.

BROWN: But he is a problem, and we expect our problems to be solved.

BLACK: You sound like a civil servant; have you had any training at all?

BROWN: No, none at all.

BLACK: You're very good.

BROWN: Thank you.

GREEN: The trouble is that I sympathise with you all, and I myself would like to see him removed. However, he has got a certain, how shall I put it, a certain advantage.

WHITE: If something is not done soon, things will get out of hand.

GREEN: In what way?

WHITE: This vicar and his open air services are becoming very popular, attracting many people.

BROWN: Sightseers in their hundreds.

WHITE: If we wait much longer, then it will be impossible to move them at all.

GREEN: I can assure you that no one appreciates the fact more than I. It used to be such a romantic spot just around there.

BLACK: Tell me something, is it not possible to use...er...more clandestine methods?

GREEN: Are you talking of subterfuge?

BLACK: I feel certain that a grateful Ministry would turn a blind eye to such methods.

GREEN: I see...as a matter of fact, a thought has occurred to me.

BLACK: Yes?

GREEN: If you could guarantee...
BLACK: Oh no, out of the question, shouldn't really be here you know.
GREEN: That's all right squire, understood...nudge' nudge eh?
BLACK: Precisely.
GREEN: You may leave it to me.
BROWN: Good...*(they all stand)* ....goodbye.
GREEN: Goodbye.

(BLACK, WHITE and BROWN exit. GREEN picks up the phone and dials a number. Phone rings off stage. BLACK, in army cap enters, with a walkie talkie)

GREEN: Captain Black?
BLACK: Speaking.
GREEN: Roger!
BLACK: Clive!
GREEN: How are you?
BLACK: Fine...you?
GREEN: Spot on...have a favour to ask.
BLACK: Fire away.
GREEN: Need a tree removed.
BLACK: No problem.
GREEN: Off the cuff, you know?
BLACK: Understood.
GREEN: No names.
BLACK: No pack drill, what?
GREEN: Spot on.
BLACK: Just need a map reference and...'boom'!
GREEN: 647, D for Dapple, A for Aubergine.
BLACK: My favourite colours.
GREEN: Thought you'd approve.
BLACK: Is that it?
GREEN: In toto.
BLACK: Wilco!
GREEN: Roger.
BLACK: Clive!

(Blackout. Sounds of marching men. The lights come up as WHITE, in army cap, marches in, halts and faces the way she entered)

WHITE: Battalion!....battalion!...keep those lines straight there...smartly, you're on parade!...*(BROWN marches in)*...battalion!....HALT!...to the front, right TURN!....steady now...RIGHT DRESS!...*(BROWN complies with all the orders)*...eyes FRONT!...that was lovely, dear.
BROWN: Oh, do you think so?
WHITE: A credit.

BROWN: Why, thank you.

BLACK: *(Entering)* Lieutenant?

WHITE: Sir!

BLACK: Battalion ready for inspection?

WHITE: Sir!...Battalion...for inspection. Open order MARCH!... *(BROWN takes two steps forward)* ready for inspection, sir.

BLACK: Thank you, Lieutenant...*(Proceeds to inspect BROWN)*...fine turn out, fine body of men.

WHITE: Thank you sir.

BLACK: *(Still circling)* Fine body.

BROWN: Thank you sir.

BLACK: Right...fall out the demolition squad if you will, Lieutenant.

WHITE: Sir!...demolition squad...fall OUT!

(BROWN takes one step forward, salutes and then breaks away to WHITE'S side)

BLACK: Are you the entire squad?

WHITE: No sir, one man still to come.

BLACK: Oh?

BROWN: He has had a tiring time, sir.

(GREEN staggers on carrying a large box. The two women spring to help him)

WHITE: There, there, did those others make you carry it all by yourself?...you should have told me.

BROWN: Let me carry it.

WHITE: No. I will.

BROWN: It's my turn.

GREEN: Bloody let go, will you.

WHITE: Come on, darling, bear up.

BLACK: Just what is going on?

GREEN: I want a bloody transfer.

BROWN: Oh no!

GREEN: It's them two, isn't it, I'm the only bloody man in this bloody demolition squad, and they won't let me alone. Keep on pawing me, and bloody touching me...look at them...bloody get off!...let go!... *(They let him go and he slumps to the ground)* I'm bloody knackered, sir, I didn't get any kip till gone four this morning.

WHITE: Four?...but you left me at...*(She glares at BROWN, who sticks her tongue out)* You poor dear, you, let me help.

GREEN: Leave me alone.

BLACK: Do you realise that's an officer you are talking to?

GREEN: I know, but they won't let me alone.

WHITE: Come along, ups a daisy.

BROWN: Up you get.

BLACK: FALL IN!... *(The two women jump to attention and GREEN slowly collapses again)* You are army, not a bunch of weak-kneed women...demolition party, to your positions, fall in!

(The women dash to the box, one takes out a large drill and fixes it together. The other takes out a detonator and plunger. They rush to the tree, kneel and take up positions either side of the tree)

WHITE: Number One squad ready and in position, sir!
BROWN: Number Two squad ready and in position, sir!
BLACK: Very good...*(points to GREEN)*...what about him?
GREEN: I'm not bloody ready.
WHITE: *(Whispers to GREEN)* Shall I...?
GREEN: *(Panics)* No, no, no, no, I'll manage, don't touch me. *(He crawls to his knees, and goes towards WHITE)* Let's have the bloody drill then.
WHITE: *(Proudly)* Well done dear. *(Tries to kiss him)*
GREEN: Get off!
BLACK: Are you ready?
GREEN: Bloody looks like it, doesn't it...*(starts to drill into the side of the tree)*
BROWN: You really ought to tell the officer that you are ready, dear.
GREEN: Bloody shut up, will you.
BROWN: But it's in standing orders, dear.
GREEN: Sod the orders!
WHITE: Driller, ready and in position, sir!
BLACK: Very well, carry on.
GREEN: I've bloody finished, haven't I?
BLACK: Already?
GREEN: The bloody tree's rotten, the bloody drill went right in without me trying.
BROWN: I do wish you wouldn't swear quite so much, dear.
WHITE: I like it.
BROWN: You've made that painfully obvious.
WHITE: Don't you talk to me that way.
BROWN: Silly cow!
WHITE: Oh!...*(stands up)*...well, you've asked for it.
BROWN: *(Standing)* Just like you did last night, outside the hut. Thought you couldn't be seen, didn't you?
WHITE: Having a cheap thrill?
BLACK: Ladies!
WHITE & BROWN: Oh, shut up!
GREEN: I'm bloody off.
BLACK: Where are you going?
GREEN: As far as I can from that bloody tree, it's liable to fall down any minute. *(MOTHER, ELSIE and CINDY enter, carrying placards showing 'Sermon from the Tree', and 'Jesus lives in the Leaves')*

WHITE: Who are they?

BLACK: Local people; they mustn't know the Army is here. Quick, mingle.

(BROWN and WHITE grab GREEN and pull him down to the ground, under the tree. BLACK sits to one side. The other women bring in a short bench, set it down and sit down, facing the tree. They all produce knitting which they commence all through the sermon. Heavenly music starts to come from the top of the tree and they gaze up in rapture. Lights fade down and a white light shines down on them from the top of the tree. The VICAR'S recorded voice is heard)

VICAR: *(Recording)* Brethren...and sisters!...I am here in the tree and my image must not be confused with that of God..well, not too much, at any road. Your selfless contributions over the past weeks will enable tree churches to be built all over the world. The Word will issue forth from ja carander, from the oak and the ash, not forgetting the bonny ivy tree. Keep the faith!...and keep the money rolling in! I shall now sing 'Nearer my God to Thee', and you will listen. *(The tape clicks and his voice is heard, singing. The light goes down and stage lights up)*

MOTHER: Wasn't that lovely?

ELSIE: Lovely.

MOTHER: A real comfort.

CINDY: Oh, he is, he is.

(Pause)

MOTHER: Sings well, doesn't he?

CINDY: Did you notice something?

MOTHER: What?

CINDY: He never mentioned Gregory again.

ELSIE: That's three weeks now, since he did.

CINDY: Do you suppose he's still up there?

ELSIE: He must be.

MOTHER: I hope he's changed his socks.

AGENT: *(Entering, rattling a collecting box)* Hullo there!

CINDY: How's Gregory?

AGENT: Who?...oh, Gregory...fine, I think.

CINDY: You think?

AGENT: Last time I spoke to him.

CINDY: Haven't you seen him?

AGENT: Only his feet.

MOTHER: What shoes did he have on?

AGENT: Brown, I think.

MOTHER: He's still got his best shoes on, the monkey.

AGENT: Well come on...*(rattles box)*...ante up.

ELSIE: What is it this week?

AGENT: Relief for Bangladesh.

ELSIE: Again?

AGENT: It's for Birmingham this time...besides, when did we have it last?

ELSIE: Two weeks ago.

AGENT: There you are then...oi'! What about you lot under the tree?

BLACK: Are you addressing me?

AGENT: That's right cocker, and what about those two randy bitches with you?

BLACK: I don't think you're going to get much out of them.

AGENT: Someone is.

VICAR: *(Entering)* I say!

AGENT: Here, what are you doing here, you're supposed to be up there, singing.

VICAR: The tape is doing that.

AGENT: You burke, I know that and you know that, but the punters don't. Remember the image.

VICAR: This is urgent.

AGENT: You should have gone before you got up there.

VICAR: I thought I heard someone crying.

AGENT: Where?

VICAR: In the tree.

AGENT: Who could it be?

VICAR: Must be that Kerslake fellow.

REPORTER: *(Rushing on)* Right, where is it?

VICAR: Where's what?

REPORTER: My exclusive story.

AGENT: What are you on about?

REPORTER: I got a message to come here and there would be a story.

AGENT: What do you think we are, bleeding Jackanory? Wasn't me.

VICAR: Nor me.

AGENT: Mind you, if you want a story...

REPORTER: What?

AGENT: It's our new idea for improving the image. We are aiming to have choirs stationed in all the trees around here. They will back the singing, in stereo of course. Imagine it, all these trees ablaze with light and sound. Should bring in the punters in thousands.

REPORTER: A sort of 'Son et Lumiere'.

AGENT: If you like.

VICAR: All my sermons will be printed, and on sale.

AGENT: We are going to have parades and ancient pageants.

VICAR: On that point, I do think that the idea of having vestal virgins maybe a shade too much.

AGENT: How's that?

VICAR: Don't seem to get the virgins these days, at least, I don't.

CINDY: What about Gregory?

AGENT: Have we got plans for that lad! We'll dress him all in sequins.

VICAR: Spotlighted in the tree. *(There is a long drawn out wail from the top of the tree, followed by a crash. Silence)*

AGENT: Oh no, don't tell me!

(BLACK, BROWN, WHITE and GREEN go round behind the tree and come out, bearing the 'corpse', in a blanket. They place it on the ground, pointing down towards the audience. Then they, and the other four, form two lines either side of the body. The VICAR walks slowly round to the head, facing the audience)

VICAR: We are gathered here today to pay tribute to a misguided youth, who sought to alter the course of progress. In doing so, many people were enmeshed into his web of intrigue.

ALL: Hallelujah!

VICAR: Because of his actions, a husband has been lost...*(CINDY begins to sob and the AGENT puts his arm round her)*

AGENT: Never you mind, love, have I got some plans for you. You'll look great in black.

CINDY: Oh no, black is not my best colour.

AGENT: I was thinking of underwear.

CINDY: Oh!

AGENT: I have this friend, see, who does calendars...not Pirelli you understand, but he makes a living.

CINDY: And does he pay well?

AGENT: You leave all that to me darling.

CINDY: Oh goody! *(they exit arm in arm)*

VICAR: Is there any way a bereaved mother can face the shock?

REPORTER: Well now, as he's snuffed it, I can at last do that story on his life, from the mother's angle, of course.

MOTHER: Do they pay well?

REPORTER: That depends.

MOTHER: On what?

REPORTER: On whether I can come up with something...certain papers will pay that much extra, for a little...extra? Know what I mean?

MOTHER: Funny you should say that, there was a certain time when I caught him, down the shed. He was all by himself, and he thought everyone else had gone to the pictures...*(they exit)*

VICAR: You see, you are bringing contentment...and what of your original thought.

BLACK: *(In bowler hat)* "As a result of the last General Election, the new Government expenditure has been revised. The new road has been shelved, for the time being".

VICAR: There, you see, Gregory, you've won after all. The police can now go about their normal duties...*(BLACK and WHITE, in police hats, put their arms round each other and run off into the bushes)*...the dogs of war need slip no more...*(BROWN grabs GREEN and drags him off)*...for my own personal sake, I am sorry that the tree churches have been denied, but that's show business for you.

ELSIE: What about me?

VICAR: Ah yes, my dear, I have been told that my voice inspires you, and in that, I am gratified. But that is not enough I fear, for beneath this cloth there exists a certain...

ELSIE: Yes?

VICAR: A certain?...what is the word?...oh yes, lust. *(he grabs her by the arm and they start to run off)*

ELSIE: *(Stopping and looking back)* What about him?

VICAR: Him?...he was human, my dear, bloody interfering, but human. Perhaps he's now got what he desired. Anyway...*(goes to the corpse)* He won't be needing this any more. *(he takes the blanket revealing the bloodstained body of GREGORY. They exit leaving the body in the spotlight. Blackout)*

CURTAIN

SOUND EFFECTS

Sound of marching men.
Heavenly music.
Tape of 'Nearer my God to thee'.

PERSONAL PROPERTIES

BROWN.	Various hats.
WHITE.	Various hats, notebook and pencil.
GREEN.	Various hats.
BLACK.	Various hats, walkie-talkie.
AGENT.	Collecting box.
REPORTER.	Notebook and pencil.

GENERAL PROPERTIES

2 small tables.
4 chairs.
Large map.
2 telephones.
Red felt-tip pen.
Table cloth.
Cutlery.
Rope.
Note.
Cabbage.
Mock drill, mock detonator and plunger.
Placards.
Bench.
Tape recorder.